Raccoon Hunting Basics and Beyond
by
Bob Rakow and Dr. Tom C. Rakow

Cover photo: Bob Rakow with Andy (a three-legged bluetick) and Baldy.

Dedicated to Marie Rakow, wife and mother.

Acknowledgments

The initial booklet *Raccoon Hunting Basics* grew out of the consistent requests for additional information made by visitors to the "Raccoon Hunting Questions" website (this site may be found by going to www.rockdove.com and following the link). We are thankful for the inspiration these questions and requests have provided. In fact, out of these questions eventually grew the audio project titled *Raccoon Hunting Questions* which covers additional subject matter that was not contained in *Raccoon Hunting Basics*.

In *Raccoon Hunting Basics and Beyond* we have taken this foundational knowledge about raccoon hunting a step further. The materials contained between the covers of this book are gleaned from literally thousands of hunts which took place under star-studded skies and span more than five decades. Not only does this newest work include and significantly elaborate on most of the material found in the original booklet, but the reader will also find helpful photos, answers to a few additional training questions, and a basic glossary of raccoon hunting terms. As an extra bonus and for your personal entertainment and enrichment we have included several raccoon hunting related devotionals. This newest book now replaces the earlier small booklet. Nevertheless, it is important to remember that this work should not be understood as a replacement for the instructional audio *Raccoon Hunting Questions*. Rather, *Raccoon Hunting Basics and Beyond* should serve as an excellent companion to the audio.

The reader will also find some biographical information about the late Bob Rakow (my dad) towards the back of this book. Bob, who went to be with the Lord in 1998 after co-authoring *Raccoon Hunting Basics,* should also be credited with much of the new material found in this book. Admittedly, almost everything I know about raccoon hunting I learned firsthand from my dad. I do not know how old I actually was the first time I went on a coon hunt. However, I do know that it was over forty years ago. Furthermore, I am thankful for each and every hunt we had together. I am also grateful for the many family members and friends with whom we enjoyed hunts. Also worthy of acknowledgement are the many gracious landowners who over the years allowed raccoon hunting on their property. Most of all, I am thankful to the God of the universe who has granted to each one of us ". . . life and breath and everything else" (Acts 17:25).

Happy Hunting!

Dr. Tom C. Rakow

Table of Contents

The Equipment You Need

The necessary materials for raccoon hunting are really quite basic. They consist of: a good dog, a bright light, an accurate .22 caliber rifle, and a sharp knife for skinning purposes. Even so, it is important to realize that every single part of this simple equation is vital.

Your Dog

Most importantly, if you don't have a dog that's able to put a raccoon up a tree or has not yet learned to let you know where the treed critter is, you have a problem! Indeed, the most time-consuming, tedious, and tenuous part of raccoon hunting is training a dog to track his or her own quarry. If raccoon hunting merely involved purchasing a few items at a local sporting goods store and then sprinting off to the nearest woods, there would be a lot more participants in this night-time activity. Yet, as you will learn later, the types of dogs that can be trained to run raccoon are not strictly confined to a certain type of hound.

Your Light

In the same way, if your dog has put a raccoon up a leafy oak (which especially occurs early in the fall) and you are unable to find it, your rifle will be useless. The key is brightness. You need to use the kind of light with which you can shine the beam high up in a tree. However, one of the advantages in using a type of head lantern is that it helps to free up a hand for holding on to a dog, carrying a rifle, or crossing fences.

Your Weapon

While the actual harvesting of a raccoon is in many cases anticlimactic, the shooting conditions under which this takes place are quite unpredictable. You may find yourself on a steep hillside, in a wet swamp, or on a rocky ridge. Furthermore, the raccoon itself might be largely concealed by leaves and limbs, on the ground fighting with your dog, or in a treetop which is being swayed with the wind.

We have used both rifles and pistols. However, a weapon with a longer barrel can often make a difficult shot much more manageable. A .22 caliber rifle with long-rifled hollow points works well. Don't use shorts. Although packing a pistol can make walking through the woods a lot easier, using a sidearm does have its drawbacks. With a pistol, there is additional space between the end of the barrel and your target. In the dark, there is always the danger of a hunting companion unknowingly stepping in front of your weapon (e.g. during one of those exciting moments when the raccoon decides to bail out of the tree). Of course, this is true regardless of the firearm being used. If your dog does catch a raccoon on the ground, you are in for an exciting time! When your dog bays a raccoon on the ground, you will want to get as close as possible before shooting. Using a rifle can help reduce the chances of your dog being injured from lunging at the raccoon and into the line of fire.

We know of one occasion when the son took his dad's hound out for a run (note: this was not Tom!). He did this despite strict orders from his father beforehand not to take the dog out while he was gone. The son disobeyed and the dog ended up catching a coon in the cornfield. During the fight the young man went to shoot the raccoon. Sadly, just as he squeezed the trigger the dog made a grab for the coon—and he killed the dog!

Remember, hunting in the dark carries some unseen or overlooked dangers. Always watch where your muzzle is pointed. Indeed, seemingly unloaded guns have killed people. There is normally no reason to actually have a shell in the chamber until the dog has treed the raccoon. Even so, regularly use your light to check the weapon's safety mechanism!

Your Knife

A knife that holds an edge will also prove helpful when it comes to removing a raccoon's hide or cutting up the carcass. For the most part, skinning is a learned skill. Nevertheless, practice should help you to become much more proficient. Later on in this book you will find some additional tips regarding this specific subject matter.

The Dog You Will Be Training

During the latter thirty-plus years of his raccoon hunting career, Bob hunted strictly with hounds. However, for more than two decades prior to this, he used a variety of dogs which included: collie crosses, a terrier, German shepherd, and even a registered springer spaniel. In fact, almost any dog that will tree squirrels can be used on raccoon. It may be that your prized family pet has raccoon hunting capabilities which could be readily developed.

Picking out, or selecting, a dog to train to hunt raccoons often requires a significant time commitment on behalf of the owner. Because of this, you will probably want to choose the kind of dog that catches on quickly. Therefore, starting with a breed traditionally recognized for running raccoon is a wise way to begin. Yet it is important to remember that just because a dog belongs to a particular breed does not necessarily mean it will or will not excel in hunting. While it is true that some breeds may have traits, temperaments, or a nose which makes some kinds of training easier (e.g. a golden retriever will generally be much easier to train to fetch than a hound), even certain pedigreed hounds may look great (e.g. if they have been bred solely for show), but can lack those innate abilities which are needed on a trail. For this reason it is best to select a breed known for running raccoon, and from established hunting stock within the breed. For example, if you know a houndsperson who is well known for getting a lot of raccoon each season—that would be a good place to start. If you don't know of anyone in your area, you might ask a local fur buyer if they know of someone who sells a significant number of hides on an annual basis. Remember, just because someone "claims" to have harvested a lot of raccoon does not make it true.

When You Should Start Training

Teaching your dog some basic obedience from the very onset, while they are still a puppy, can help in the overall training process. Indeed, just getting your dog to come or get into a kennel or crate before going on an actual hunt will probably save you a whole lot of frustration later. Looking for or playing tag with your young dog in the dark when you're either ready to go home or onto another hunting spot gets old quite quickly.

How can you teach a dog to come and then load up when you want? One method for teaching such behavior is to make your dog learn that you are always in control. If possible, take your dog to an area which is enclosed (e.g. a high school football field or baseball park). Take a long rope such as a cloth clothesline and tie it on your dog's collar. Let the dog run, but maintain control of the rope. Call your dog just before you tug on the rope, and then gently but firmly reel the dog in. Continue to repeat this until your dog begins to realize that you are in control regardless of where he or she may be in the enclosure. Reward your dog with verbal praise (and even a treat) when he or she responds. Of course teaching a dog to come when called should ideally be done when your dog is still a pup. Just remember to call your dog by name just prior to "reeling" him or her in on the rope. And, always praise your dog for the appropriate response.

But what if your dog fails (or refuses) to get into the portable kennel or crate? How can you encourage your dog to load up? This can and should also be taught while your dog is in the puppy stage. Initially you may want to toss a little treat into the crate or kennel in which you haul your dog. Practice having your dog go in and out of the kennel on command. Do not leave the dog shut up for an extended period of time. All training (especially when your dog is a pup) should be kept short, simple, and sweet. Keep all training sessions brief, and end them in a positive fashion. Extending a training session too long will start to sour your dog.

When it comes to actual hunting, we have found that a pup normally needs to be at least six months old before it can begin to catch on to chasing raccoon. Yet, even if a puppy starts putting raccoon up, it will still need to do a lot of maturing before he or she develops into a "seasoned" coon dog. In the field, introducing an eight to ten month-old dog will normally prove to be far more productive with regard to seeing real returns on your training-time investment.

Frequently a dog that is six to nine months old (or even older) will not want to leave your side—or will stay close on your heels when walking. This can be frustrating or even embarrassing if you are hunting with someone who has well-seasoned dogs. While your friend's dogs are running raccoon, your dog is hanging tight. However, such behavior is quite common and should normally be expected of a young dog.

How does one deal with a dog that refuses to range out? Initially you may want to take your dog by the collar and try coaxing (or gently thrusting) your dog into a cornfield you may be walking alongside. If and when your dog returns, do the same thing over a couple more times. If the dog returns—simply ignore your dog. Try to not pat or praise your dog if they come right back to you. You do not want to further encourage such unwanted behavior. Instead, just ignore your dog.

Your dog will eventually begin ranging out further and further from you. Nevertheless, from time to time your dog may revert back to this type of "juvenile" behavior and want to stay close.

If you are training your canine with a mature coon dog, what usually happens is when the trained dog starts running or treeing then the younger dog will periodically start to join in—although he/she at first will probably not bark on the trail nor at the tree. Due to apparent curiosity or perhaps pack instinct, your dog may just range out a little from you, but then quickly return without even joining in on the chase. However, don't be discouraged!

At the tree your young dog may run around in an excited or even confused fashion, but not join in on the treeing. Furthermore, your dog may not seem interested in chewing or mouthing the raccoon after it has been harvested. Again, don't be discouraged because for a young dog this lack of interest is often quite normal.

We have found that most often a dog (even started at a young age) will begin showing real maturity on the trail and at the tree when they are around two-and-a-half to three years-of-age. At around four or five years a dog that has been hunting consistently will often have arrived at his or her peak. This is not to say that they will quit learning. However, observable improvements in your dog's raccoon hunting ability will probably be minimal. In addition, in the next couple of years, your dog's physical agility and endurance capability will gradually begin to decline.

Remember that good training often takes a great deal of time. It's sort of like a youngster just learning how to read. They first begin identifying letters of the alphabet, then a few words may start being sounded out. After a while, short phrases or groups of words are linked together. But then, almost magically, at some point it begins to "click." Therefore, try to be patient with your dog and don't always expect to see immediately discernable results.

A simulated hunt allows you the opportunity to see your dog at work during the daylight hours. Pictured above are a couple of blueticks (Skipper and Baldy) treeing on a raccoon hide.

A Simulated Hunt

A "simulated hunt" is an attempt to develop a dog's basic skills so that it may eventually run and tree a raccoon. Of primary importance in a simulated hunt is the scent of a raccoon.

To set up this type of mock hunt, an individual can use a fresh road kill, raccoon hide, or commercial scent. Some people may be in a position to use a tame coon or so-called "lead coon" to make a trail. It should be noted that in certain states picking up road kill may be illegal unless you have a special license—so be sure to check your state's hunting regulations.

As far as a raccoon hide goes, you will probably be able to purchase one from an area fur buyer or, better yet, skin out a road kill. A hide that is frozen need not be thawed out for every training session. After using it on a simulated hunt, simply return the hide to a bag and put it in the freezer. Remember that if you do choose to keep a hide in a plastic bag in a freezer for training or storage purposes, be careful not to contaminate any food.

Raccoon scent can usually be ordered through ads in appropriate hunting magazines. Smaller quantities, which are used by some archery hunters as a type of "cover scent," will be found in many sporting goods stores or departments. Apply this to a rag or cloth and drag with a rope or string.

When you first lay a trail, try to keep it short and simple. The hide should not be openly visible to the dog. As your dog catches on, you will probably want to make the run more complex. However, try not to always run the trail to the same tree. In order to prevent confusing your dog (especially in the early stages), avoid laying a trail across one they have just finished running. If you use a road kill or a hide, let the dog smell and shake it some while you verbally praise him or her during the process. For example, you can have a rope on the hide and toss the hide on a low or flat roof out of the dog's view. After the dog takes the trail up to the house and begins treeing, you can then pull the hide down. Encourage your dog to grab hold by pulling the hide around with the rope. Praise the dog as he or she shakes the hide. After a minute or two say something like, "OK, that's enough!" Then take the hide away and praise your dog some more. Remember to keep these training sessions short and enjoyable. Always leave your dog wanting more! It is better if you can use a hide in conjunction with scent rather than just scent alone. Being able to run, tree, and then being able to mouth the hide will serve as a source of positive reinforcement for your dog.

Don't become alarmed if your dog does not stay precisely on the trail you have laid out for him or her. While it is true that certain dogs will track a raccoon by strictly following the trail, others will wind the trail you have laid.

Winding the trail you have established may involve the dog running down wind from the trail or making circles. Your dog may very well use a combination of both these two methods.

A simulated hunt is helpful in that it introduces your dog to the raccoon scent in a more controlled and convenient environment. A simulated hunt can be done during the daylight hours which also affords you the opportunity to see your dog in action. You may also find it easier to get your dog used to barking at the tree after it has smelled and seen an actual hide. Nevertheless, a simulated hunt is still not the "real thing," but rather good preparation for an actual hunt.

Bob Rakow with Andy (who later lost a
leg) and an evening catch of raccoon.
Notice the black raccoon.

An Actual Hunt

Getting your dog involved in an actual raccoon hunt
is key. It may mean hunting on your own in an area
where raccoons are known to be causing damage or ask-
ing another hunter if you and your dog can go along. In
either case, the goal is to give your dog some first-hand
exposure as to what it should be chasing.

Remember to get permission to hunt and let the
landowner know when you will be there. Even then, a
coon dog can easily end up on posted property. Avoid
hunting too close to such areas as well as next to busy
highways.

Where to Hunt

An ideal place in the part of the country where most
of our hunting has been done would include an unpicked
cornfield with a stream or pond nearby and oak trees.
However, raccoon can be found in a variety of places.
The time of year and the food sources available will influ-
ence the place you hunt. Swamps are great places for
raccoon, but they can also be difficult places for humans
to hunt. It's not much fun tramping through a wet

swamp at midnight!

During the first part of the season a grove of oak trees can often yield a good run or two. Choke cherries are also a favorite food. In time a successful raccoon hunter will have their favorite spots to hunt. He or she will also learn the best way to approach an area. If your dog has run a raccoon to a den tree a time or two, you may want to switch your approach. Instead of beginning at the corn field where they are feeding, start by hunting away from the tree or rock den.

Raccoon love sweet corn, and most people don't realize how quickly a crop can be damaged, or even totally destroyed, by a large concentration of wildlife. I know I didn't despite having grown up on a dairy farm and having spent many years involved with agriculture. It wasn't until a vegetable canning company that I worked for as a field supervisor had problems with raccoons. I watched as a large field of sweet corn located next to a state park in Wisconsin (where no hunting is allowed) was for the most part decimated in just a few short nights. The raccoon population certainly must have been enormous. And, raccoons seem to know when sweet corn is ready. Perhaps worst of all, they destroyed as much, or even more, than they ate. They often go through a field, climb a stalk until it bends over or breaks, then, after they take a bite or two out of the middle of an ear, they go on to another nearby cornstalk.

In this particular case, the Department of Natural Resources was contacted and quickly installed towers with horns that would blast at about every half hour after dark. This seemed to work one night, but the raccoon quickly became conditioned—and then ignored the noisy horns. The company I worked for had no other choice than to harvest the crop prematurely before the crop was entirely lost.

It should be pointed out that if wildlife is not kept in proper check, severe consequences can result. Those who think that hunting should be banned often fail to realize ways in which uncontrolled wildlife populations can affect the environment and the future of a wildlife population itself. Diseases can spread and decimate herds or flocks which have become overpopulated. Vegetation can be destroyed and predators can begin wreaking havoc on nesting areas—including those of threatened or endangered species. Indeed, predators are not prejudiced in that they will eat the offspring of threatened species as well as any other. Furthermore, agricultural crops upon which individual landowners and local rural economies are dependent can also suffer severe damage.

Hunting along Rivers

Hunting along large rivers can be very productive, but can also involve some major problems. First of all, if the raccoon crosses the river and your dogs follow, you will need to get across. If the water is deep and wide you may have to travel a great distance on foot before crossing.

There is also a chance your dog may put a raccoon up a tree that hangs out over the river. When you shoot the raccoon out of the tree it will probably drop in the water. If the current is strong you may have an extremely difficult time retrieving the animal.

Another problem with hunting along a river is that your dog may wind up fighting with a raccoon in the water. An older raccoon can be pretty ferocious when caught by a dog on the ground, and even more so when water is involved! It makes for a scary scene with water splashing, a dog barking, the raccoon snarling, and lights reflecting.

There is a common saying among raccoon hunters, "A coon can drown a dog." Although I would not be surprised if this can or has happened, it must be a rather rare occurrence. In fact, after decades of hunting it has never happened to us, nor do we know of anyone who has actually lost a dog due to drowning by a raccoon.

Hunting on Your Own

When hunting on your own, it's important to hit an area that has a heavy concentration of raccoon. For example, if someone you know has been having trouble with raccoon raiding their garden, sweet corn patch, or getting into their garbage cans, these places should be considered "hot spots."

Hunting when there is a lot of dew on the ground and grass or after a rain can greatly help a young dog pick up a trail. Getting your dog started on a "hot track" is important. A young dog will not only have an easier time keeping on a fresh trail, it will also be more likely to complete the run. Moreover, if your dog is right behind a raccoon when it goes up a tree, the mere excitement is liable to result in spontaneous treeing. If this happens, you have not only given your hound some practical trailing experience, you can also coax, encourage, and thereby train, an already excited dog to keep on barking and treeing.

Running Your Dog with Someone Else's Dog

If you are privileged to go along on a hunt with someone else, be sensitive to his or her hunting wishes. This may mean keeping your dog tied up until the experienced dog strikes. Of course, leading a young excited hound through a tangled cornfield is no easy task. Even so, you don't want your dog to interfere with another dog's attempt to straighten out or warm up the trial.

Instead of charging ahead to the tree when the raccoon has been put up, you will want to follow behind your host. Use your light only when it is necessary or as it seems appropriate. Few things can be more frustrating to an individual who normally hunts alone than having somebody along shining their beam every which way. Remember that you are the guest and will most likely want to go along on another hunt. Don't ruin your chances!

Furthermore, the experience your dog will receive is extremely valuable. So, even if your dog participates in running and treeing a coon, don't anticipate getting a percentage of what is treed.

Perhaps most of all, never violate your host's hospitality by hunting the very same places where they have taken you. Treat them as you would want to be treated. Keep in mind that your host hunter is doing you a big favor by helping to get your dog running on the right track.

There are certainly many advantages in running your dog with somebody else's. However, there are also a few disadvantages. For example, an individual needs to make sure that one's host dog does not run trash. It would be unfortunate to unknowingly train your dog to start running the wrong kind of game. A couple of bad runs can ruin a dog that may have had great potential. Don't just assume that because your best friend says that he or she has one of the greatest hounds to ever live, that it's necessarily true. Hunt with someone in the area who is known for having good, sound coon dogs.

Keeping Your Dog on the Right Track

A major concern for any raccoon hunter is that his or her dog is chasing what it is supposed to be chasing. Do what you can to get your dog started on the right track—and then do what you can to keep him or her "straight."

Probably every hound that we ever trained eventually had a run-in with a skunk. Even so, Mr. Skunk usually does a pretty powerful job of making this a very unpleasant experience (for both dog and owner)! This is especially so if the dog gets a good shot in the mouth or eyes. The dog sometimes vomits, rolls in the grass, etc. Seldom will a dog take up tracking skunks full-time, although (perhaps due to memory lapse) your dog may periodically give a repeat performance of such behavior. If your coon dog rides in the car—as opposed to a box in the back of the truck, the trip home from a night of hunting will certainly prove to be a memorable one!

On the other hand, a dog that gets started chasing deer is a completely different story. Such behavior should not be left unchecked. If your dog does happen to bounce into a deer, try to immediately stop the chase with a verbal command. However, if your dog doesn't stop when you call, then attempt to head him or her off at the pass by getting between the deer and the dog. Never over-discipline a dog, but with such behavior an owner needs to be firm for the dog's sake. Although we have never used one, some hunters find a shock collar can be helpful in curbing such activity. In certain states, a dog that is seen in pursuit of a deer risks being shot.

It is far better if your dog never gets started running deer. To help avoid ending up with a deer-runner, don't unnecessarily tempt your dog by hunting in an area that has an excessive concentration of deer or hunt during the peak deer rut in your area. An older dog that has proven to strictly hunt raccoon may be trusted in such situations. Nevertheless, a young dog especially needs to be kept in control and not allowed to get started running deer. In this case, the old adage proves true that states, "an ounce of prevention is worth a pound of cure."

George (above) first began treeing his own raccoon at six months of age. However, this is certainly the exception rather than the rule!

Treeing

Getting your dog to bark at the appropriate tree and then to continue barking until you arrive can be a difficult hurdle to overcome. Furthermore, some dogs develop at a slower pace than do others when it comes to this area. Barking on the trail is one thing, but barking at the end of the trail is another matter altogether.

Indeed, there are dogs that, while in the process of running a raccoon, will end up doing little or no barking. This is fine because an absence of barking can actually enable a dog to get closer to a coon and thereby put it up a tree quicker. Coon dogs that do this are commonly called "silent trailers." Yet, even a silent trailer needs to learn how to tree.

Once your dog has actually treed, it is important that a significant amount of time be spent urging him or her to continue barking. Encouraging your dog to bark at the tree can usually be done by simply slapping or patting the tree and verbally praising your dog as it barks. Although you may want to hurry on for the next run, take this opportunity to help reinforce the need for your dog to keep barking until you come to the location where it has treed.

Running your dog with another more experienced dog can be extremely helpful in getting the treeing process started. For one thing, your dog might automatically join in on the barking. For another, even if your dog doesn't bark at a tree where a coon has been put up, you are still in a position to be able to help train your dog to do so.

A Bell on Your Dog's Collar

A key to keeping your dog at the tree until you get there is your being nearby when and where the coon goes up. For the most part, this is much easier said than done. However, one way a person can get to the tree more quickly is by tying a small bell on the dog's collar. In this fashion, a person can better monitor the dog's movements. If you begin to sense the dog is onto something, be alert and seek to stay as close as you can to the sound of the bell. Usually a dog's excitement on a trail is indicated by such things as: exuberant tail wagging, intensified loud sniffing, yipping, racing back and forth in a corn row, etc.

If your dog leaves a cornfield, pond area, or creek, and begins heading toward a stand of trees, you might need to pay special attention. Should the sound of the bell seem to stay in a particular part of the woods, your dog may have found or put a raccoon up a tree. You will want to check some of the trees in the general vicinity where you have been hearing the bell. It could simply be that your dog has not yet caught onto the treeing aspect.

Even using a bell with an experienced, older dog can come in handy when hunting in windy conditions. For example, in a noisy cornfield located on a ridge, you will normally have a better idea which way your dog may have headed. Although it may affect the solitude of the hunt, we have found that the sound of the bell doesn't seem to negatively interfere with the outcome of the chase.

Barking on Command

Teaching your dog to bark on command can be helpful if used during either a simulated hunt or at the tree in an actual hunt. Furthermore, this is something that even a very young dog can be taught quite easily.

You can do this by using a little bit of food and a sign (e.g. wiggle your finger and say, "speak"). When your dog barks in response to your signal, reward this desired behavior by giving your dog the food. After awhile, you can wean your dog off of the treat and replace it with verbal praise. In psychological terms, this is referred to as positive reinforcement. This controlled stimulus (CS) helps produce the controlled response (CR). In this case, the food is the CS and the barking is the CR.

Training your dog to bark on command can help make encouraging a quiet or hesitant dog to bark at the tree a much simpler task. Though your dog will still have to associate the need to bark at the exact tree in which the raccoon has been put up, at least part of your problem will have been solved.

Premature Barking

There are occasions when a dog will let out a few barks up a tree before actually settling down and confidently treeing where the raccoon has gone up. In fact, even the most experienced coon dog will sometimes "tap a tree." This seems to happen for a number of reasons. Sometimes a raccoon may start up a tree and then come back down before going up another tree. Or, the dog may just be making sure that the trail does not continue on. There might also be more than one raccoon. If your dog should happen to "tap a tree" or two before it starts treeing confidently, you will probably want to come back and check to see if additional raccoon have also been put up.

A hunter can confuse his or her coon hunting canine by rushing in and shining the light up in the trees before the dog has settled down to treeing. The best thing to do is be quiet and wait patiently until the dog seems thoroughly convinced it has the correct tree.

Learning to "read" a dog's behavior comes with experience. Even though each dog is different, over time you will probably be able to pretty much tell what your dog is up to by the way it acts or how it barks.

Keeping Track of Your Dog

Normally when raccoon hunting a person walks with his or her dog through or along the edge of a cornfield, by a pond, or in a grove of oaks. Unless your dog is young, it will probably range out from you a ways and then periodically (perhaps every five to ten minutes) come back to where you are or, as we commonly call it, "check back in." In the event your dog does not "check back in," try calling or whistling. If the dog is close by, it will most likely return. If it is at a tree or on a trail, it might let out a bark. Sometimes it's helpful to shine your flashlight or head lantern a little as a means of indicating to your dog where you are. If your dog is in another part of the woods or at the other end of the cornfield, he or she will probably start heading your way. A young dog sometimes has a difficult time getting through a woven wire fence. If this is the case, as you call the dog, it may start yipping or barking—and you might need to return to help it over or through the fence.

However, if your dog starts running a trail and then fails to return, it may simply be that the dog is out of your hearing range. If this happens, walk in the direction you last heard the dog. He or she might be on the other side of a hill or in a nearby hollow barking up a tree. Even hearing a hound that has a good voice can prove to be a problem if you happen to be hunting on a windy night.

If you find it necessary (after having exhausted all efforts to locate your dog) to leave your four-legged hunting companion behind, be sure to return as soon as possible. We suggest leaving your hunting jacket either near where your vehicle was parked or where you initially began the hunt (e.g. spread it out just inside a couple of cornrows). The dog may backtrack and curl up on your clothes waiting for you to return. If this fails, the next step may involve contacting farmers or land owners to see if the dog has shown up at their buildings. Please note: we suggest not telephoning them at 2:00 or 3:00 in the morning!

Because an owner can easily become separated from his or her dog, it's a good idea to at least have a phone number or some other form of readable identification on the collar. In order to guard against theft, you may also opt to have your dog permanently marked. We suggest you contact a local veterinarian to discuss such possibilities.

Above a bluetick (George) and a black and tan (Blackjack) both mouth a dead raccoon after it has been shot out of the tree.

Harvesting the Raccoon

As with many forms of hunting—the kill is often anti-climatic. Once a raccoon has been treed it is important to let your dog bark for a period of time before shooting it out of the tree. Even if you are able to find the raccoon right away—encourage the dog to keep barking. This is one of the best ways to help instill in your dog the need to stay at the tree, and to continue barking until you arrive.

Sometimes, especially in a tree with lots of leaves, a raccoon can be hard to find. However, don't be in too big of a hurry to assume that no coon is present. You will want to look the tree over thoroughly. Go around the tree and shine branches and crotches from various angles. Often you will catch the reflection of an eye, or see a suspicious looking clump. In addition, frequently you will find more than one raccoon up the same tree. The fact is, the more confidence you have in your dog, the longer you will be inclined to look for the raccoon.

Of course, if the tree is hollow and the raccoon has gone in the hole you will need to call your dog off the tree before you can continue hunting. If this is the case, praise your dog briefly and then say, "Let's go!" and walk away from the tree. In order to prevent your dog from immediately returning to the tree, call or lead your dog a considerable distance from the tree or den before continuing on with the hunt.

When shooting the raccoon out of the tree it is important to make a clean kill shot to the head. Depending upon the tree, you may want to pull your dog back away from the tree before shooting. A big coon dropping thirty or more feet out of the top of a tree could seriously injure your dog.

As soon as the raccoon hits the ground, release your dog. In time (especially if your dog catches up with a raccoon in the cornfield!) your dog will learn to go for the throat. It is important to let your dog mouth the dead raccoon for a minute or so as a means of positive reinforcement. Once you decide that your dog has had an adequate amount of time to mouth the raccoon say, "That's enough!" and pull the raccoon away. If your dog persists, say, "No!" and then encourage your dog to go on and get another one.

You shouldn't be surprised or discouraged if initially your dog is hesitant (or even afraid) to grab a hold of the coon. This will come in time. If there is one common theme that we see over and over again, it is that individuals are not patient when it comes to training their dog. It literally takes years to develop a seasoned coon dog.

The two authors (Bob on the left and Tom on the right) with many of the hides harvested during the 1971 Wisconsin hunting season. Tom is holding a bluetick female named Queenie—by far the best coon dog he ever hunted with!

The Hide

Once you have harvested a raccoon, you will want to either remove the hide or get the raccoon to someone who can. If you have never skinned a raccoon, an experienced hunter in the area will more than likely be willing to show you how. Recipes on how to prepare raccoon meat can be found in wild game sections of some cookbooks. Although not always eaten, some of the ways it may be prepared include: smoking, roasting, and grinding into burgers. The meat needs to be properly cleaned, prepared, and thoroughly cooked.

The actual skinning process is much easier if it's done while the carcass is still warm. Hang the animal upside-down. Make an incision down the inside of one leg and continue up the inside of the other. Then take and cut the hide all the way around on both legs next to the feet at the point where the inside incision either began or ended. Pull down as you slice the hide away from the carcass. For the inexperienced, the tail is especially tricky to skin without breaking it off. Also, be careful when cutting around the ears and nose. Please note that the ears and nose should come off with the hide and not remain on the carcass. On the following pages you will find a series of step-by-step photos to help you begin the skinning process and to get you past the trickiest part of skinning the tail. Remember to be patient!

After the hide has been removed, it can be stretched or frozen. Freezing is generally an easier way to go. To freeze a hide, simply turn it fur-out and then roll from head to tail so that the tail is on the outside. Put it in a plastic bag and place in a freezer. Again, be careful not to put the hide where food may become contaminated. And, make sure the hide is well wrapped, or even double wrapped (e.g. in two bags), to protect it during storage in the freezer.

Frozen hides will normally be thawed enough to be taken to a fur buyer if removed from the freezer and spread out separately on newspapers or a piece of plastic the afternoon or evening before you plan on selling them. We suggest that you talk to potential fur buyers and see how they prefer hides to be brought. You will also need to study your state's hunting regulations to see what stipulations apply when it comes to transporting skins.

1. Hang the raccoon at a comfortable height.

2. Cut around both feet, and inside from leg to leg.

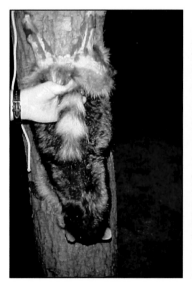

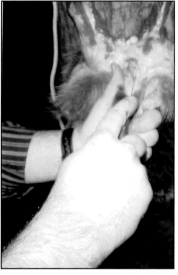

3. Pull the hide from the legs down to the tail.

4. At the base of the tail cut down along the bone.

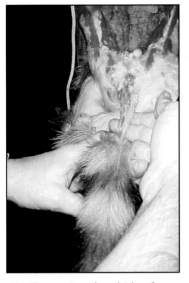

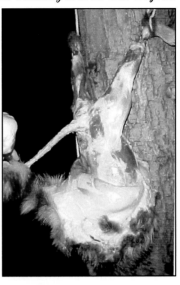

5. Separate the hide from the tail.

6. Continue to cut or pull the hide down the tail.

7. Carefully strip the hide off the entire tail.

8. Pull, being careful not to slice the hide itself.

It is important to remember that the value of a raccoon hide is affected by an important set of variables. The demand for hides can depend upon the attitude of the general public. However, the size of the hide and what time of the year the raccoon was harvested can also play a major role. Raccoon taken late in the season are normally of better quality. Prices may fluctuate some depending on when you choose to sell them. How well the raccoon was skinned and then cared for is also very important.

Hides that have been frozen and stored in a freezer can be spread out on a clean surface to thaw the day before you plan on selling.

SOME RACCOON HUNTING QUESTIONS
(Questions have been edited for the reader's benefit.)

QUESTION

My boyfriend and I have been coon hunting for almost two years and recently bought a Walker. She is a year old and very sweet, but very skittish. The man that we bought her from sent her away to be trained. The man that trained her said that she was treeing. But we have a problem getting her to load up in the truck and also getting her to go in the woods. We have had her for almost three weeks now and have taken her out almost four nights a week. She has been in the woods a few times, but we have to lead her in. Tried her with a friend's black and tan and even by herself. For a dog that has supposedly been trained she hasn't done anything. She acts as if she has no clue. Took her to a treeing competition and a coon scared her. What can we do to get her going in the right direction?

Jen

ANSWER

Jen,

You're right to question whether the dog was really trained. One of the things I make mention of on the *Raccoon Hunting Questions* tape is if you are buying a dog that is supposed to be trained, be sure and go on at least a hunt or two. That way you better know what you are getting into. Your dog may have been partially started—but certainly not trained.

The good news is that your dog is young—and can still be trained. While we had a dog that began running and treeing his own coon at six months—that is the exception rather than the rule (regardless of what others may say!).

Another piece of good news is that your dog being

skittish can actually help prevent her from being picked up—or stolen in the future. You need to teach your dog to kennel up when you want. Teach her in the daylight and make it a positive experience for her (e.g. throw a treat in the kennel—and then praise her when she responds).

QUESTION

I have a bluetick hound and I just wanted to know if I let her loose in the yard would she come to me. She is a two year old and has been used two seasons. My friend gave her to me. She knows her name. I've run her two times and she'll tree great. We live next to a main road in the country.

Jake

ANSWER

Jake,

Don't let your dog loose (especially near a highway) if you are not sure she will come to you. She will need to learn how to come to you if she doesn't now. Take her to a safe place (e.g. a football or baseball field that is fenced) and have a long, long rope (e.g. 100 foot cloth clothesline rope) which will allow you to catch her. When she responds positively—reward her (e.g. with food and praise).

QUESTION

Hi, my boyfriend has been coon hunting with friends and believes he's ready to have a coonhound of his own. I want to buy one for him, but I'm not sure what kind to get and I don't want to get ripped off. Any suggestions? I was leaning towards a beagle? Would they be okay for this?

Amanda

ANSWER

Amanda,

I would not recommend a beagle for coon hunting. While it is true that almost any dog can be taught to hunt coon, some breeds are much better suited. You could see with what breeds his friends hunt. Or, I would suggest one of the following: bluetick, redbone, treeing walker, or black and tan.

QUESTION

I saw the movie *Where a Red Fern Grows*. It was a lot about coon hunting. I remember I was surprised that the boy had to have the dog tree the coon, then cut down the tree to get the coon. Was this the way to do it back then or were they just too poor to afford a gun or are you not supposed to use a gun for some reason? Just wondering. Seemed like a lot of work for one skin.

Roxanne

ANSWER

Roxanne,

My dad who was born during the Great Depression—and was dirt poor—did not chop down trees. And, apart from the movie, I have never seen or known of this being done. In addition—it would be very difficult to harvest the coon. Normally a .22 rifle is used.

QUESTION

We have a Walker female about eight months old. She can work trails real well, but won't bark on a trail or at a tree. We've worked her on scent trails and on live caged coons, but she just won't bark. We are fifteen and fourteen and this is our first dog. We'd really hate to have a dud. PLEASE ANSWER.

Wilevan

ANSWER

Wilevan,

Your dog is not a dud! Your dog is young and there are several ways to help get her treeing.

1) Run your dog with a seasoned dog. But since this evidently is not possible you can do #2.

2) Teach her to tree on command—and then use the same principle at the tree in conjunction with a bell on your dog's collar.

QUESTION

I have a brother and sister pair of six-month-old redbones, my first coon dogs. I am inclined to get them spayed and neutered so as to prevent "complications," as I do not have separate kennels. Does fixing affect a dogs hunting characteristics? Also, I am a Wilderness First Responder and have toyed with the idea of training them as search and rescue dogs. Do you think I could train my dogs to track people as well as coon hunt?

Burger

ANSWER

Burger,

Good to hear from you! I can only speak in a general sense regarding having your dogs spayed or neutered. Your male will probably be a little less aggressive (which is okay) and may not range out quite as far as he normally would (which is also okay—this is a major reason why I prefer females). With the female it shouldn't make much difference.

As far as training your dog for the dual purpose, it is certainly possible. I would suggest that you make your training exercises very distinct from one another. For example, you may want to use a harness as opposed to a collar when training for rescue. And, only use the collar when training to coon hunt. The key would be consistency so that the dog knows what he/she is supposed to be doing. However, this can be a very difficult task because training a dog for one or the other is tough enough. You might consider using one dog for coon hunting and the other for rescue. In that way you could enjoy your dog in both worlds.

QUESTION

Just wondering what the best way is to start coon hunting. I'm a college student in North Carolina and I just adopted a six-year-old bluetick this summer. I've been a duck and dove hunter for the past three years and with this dog I'd like to start coon hunting. I just don't know how to start. In terms of where to start, my family's got an old farm that fits perfectly. I've noticed that my bluetick has a noticeable desire to hunt because if I'm not entertaining her, her nose is always in the dirt trying to track something. I've let her roam a few times and when she's gone I can tell when she's on a scent and when she's not due to her distinct howling voice. I'd love to have some good pointers for a rookie, thanks a bunch.

Stew

ANSWER

Stew,

Although your dog is pretty old to start coon hunting, he will still be able to get a few. The key is to take him where you know there are coon. A damp night would be best. Coon seem to love these nights and the tracking is easier and seems hotter. This will get your dog more excited if he gets on a raccoon trail. If the farm has a cornfield by a stream or there are some old trees near a cornfield you will probably bump into one there. Raccoon often end up near, or even under, old buildings.

QUESTION

I know this is a coon hunting site but I couldn't find anywhere else to ask this question. I'm getting two beagle puppies—brothers. I want them strictly for squirrel hunting. How do I go about training them to squirrel hunt? Is training dogs to squirrel hunt similar to training them to coon hunt? Will a beagle tree a squirrel? Thanks!

Keith

ANSWER

Keith,

Squirrel dogs almost always tree by sight. They chase them after seeing them. Raccoon hunting and squirrel hunting are similar in that the dogs in both cases should bark at the tree (raccoon at night and squirrel during the day). The primary difference is that in raccoon hunting the dog is following a scent trail at night rather than a squirrel by sight during the day.

To train them to tree squirrels, you can run them with another squirrel dog or take them to a place where they will see squirrels and run them.

QUESTION

I have gotten a nine-month-old bluetick. I have been taking him out a few times a week and all he does is whine and whimper. Is that a good sign? He has been running with an older dog and it is helping a little.

Erin

ANSWER

Erin,

Your dog is young and has a lot to learn—and is still adjusting to going out. Assuming the dogs you are running him with are good dogs, that is the best way to get your dog started. You need to be patient. Although I do remember one of our dogs was treeing his own coon at six months of age—that is not the norm. Usually the most effective time to start training on actual coon is at eight to nine months. So you are off to a good start. You might consider conducting some short simulated hunts with your dog. Again, you need to be patient. We always considered a hound (even one that was treeing its own coon) a pup until they were two to two-and-a-half years of age.

QUESTION

I have a two-year-old black and tan male that is really starting to click. He is normally good-natured, but after the coon is shot out of the tree and he sees it is dead, he gets possessive and growls over it with other dogs. What's the problem and how should I break him? Thanks!

Alan

ANSWER

Alan,

You will need to nip this in the bud right away before it gets worse. Although it is normal for this to start happening—you must not let it progress. You are in charge. Let him mouth the coon briefly. Then, take the coon away from him—and when he trees to go after it again (and he will), say "NO!" in a firm fashion. And, make sure you enforce this. After awhile he will become less resistant, and will learn that there is a time to grab the coon—and there is a time to get back to hunting. Remember you are the master. If you don't stop this behavior, he will be growling at you next.

QUESTION

How old should my treeing walker pup get before I

start training her to run and tree coons?

ANSWER

Training usually starts being productive at about ten weeks (although dogs can certainly learn at eight weeks). As far as hunting—usually around six months a pup can start catching on. Some dogs can tree their own coon at six months, but even then they are a long way from being trained. For many dogs the most productive time for starting is about eight or nine months.

QUESTION

I have a walker dog. She will be four. I just got her about two months ago and my understanding is that she has not been hunted much and she got a very bad beating for treeing a possum. Now she will hunt and tree, but she will not stay on tree very long unless she can see the coon. What can I do? Also, sometimes she will hold the tree until we get there, then she will leave. She is out of good stock. That's what everybody tells me. Please help.

ANSWER

One of the things you will want to work on is encouraging her on the tree—and prolonging the time you spend at the tree before actually shooting the coon out (especially if the trail was hot). You can also try to teach her to bark on command. Of course this can be done much more easily on a young dog.

But, if the dog knows to sit—or even kennel-up or load-up on command—then you will be able to teach her to bark on command. If you think she is going to the tree without barking, you might try putting a bell on her collar. In this way you will know the direction she went— and be able to head toward her even before she starts treeing.

QUESTION

I have recently bought a walker with a very exceptional pedigree. I was told she was started on caged coon, but I have a feeling that she has never been outside of the yard. She is one-and-a-half years old and shows potential on scent drags and trees fairly well on lead coon. My question is: will starting her training so late in her life affect her drive to hunt? Or will all that time as a yard dog give her reason to think that she is one (a yard dog)? Thanks!

Keath

ANSWER

Keath,

You are not too late. However, it is important that you really start investing time in the dog now. Although it is nice to begin working with a dog earlier—it sounds like your dog has plenty of innate ability which has already begun to show itself. Sometimes dogs can have all kinds of training, but really don't click until they are two plus years.

QUESTION

My grandfather recently got two eight-week-old blueticks. He and I have been rabbit hunting for a while and we are training the dogs for rabbit right now. However, as I find out more and more about coon hunting, I have an interest in it. I was wondering if it was possible to train the dogs to hunt both rabbits and coons (rabbits by day, coons by night). If so, how will the dogs differentiate and know what animal they're suppose to be tracking when we take them out to hunt either rabbit or coons, or would it just be best to get another dog just for coon hunting? Another question, the two blueticks are brothers and now they sleep in the same pen together. One is kind of shy and the other one is bold. They depend on each other for everything. I was wondering if it would be best for them to have separate pens to build individuality.

Jordan

ANSWER
Jordan,

If you want to hunt rabbits, hunt rabbits—or raccoon, then hunt raccoon. It will not work to hunt both with the same dogs. Although, it is possible to train a bird dog to hunt raccoon at night—the same is not true with rabbits. Your dogs will (for all practical purposes) be worthless as coon dogs and I would discourage anyone from running their dog with yours in that your dogs would probably have their dogs running rabbits as well. The key is to try and have a "straight" dog—by this I mean a dog that runs only raccoon. You could possibly train one to hunt rabbits and one to hunt raccoon.

However, you would never be able to hunt them together. Dogs will almost always establish their own pecking order regardless of how they may be housed. One dog will end up being dominate.

QUESTION
What do you think about coon hunting in the snow? Is it a good time or not? When is the best time? Thanks!

Kevin

ANSWER
Kevin,

It is possible to hunt raccoon in the snow. However, the time to do this is when there is a warm-up. Otherwise they stay holed up in their den. The runs are also often quite short.

QUESTION

I live on a dairy farm in Virginia and we own about 1,500 acres of land, but not all of it is woods. I have about five or six good spots to hunt. I would have tons more spots to hunt, but I have a river that runs through my farm and I don't want my dogs to get drowned. I have a eight-month-old plott and a six-year-old bluetick. (I'm trying to train the plott, without a whole lot of success so far.) Anyway, I was wondering if it's bad to hunt the same areas more than once every couple of weeks or so. If you can tell me, I would appreciate it much.

Brent

ANSWER

Brent,

As long as the spots are producing, it is fine. You may want to try entering these hot spots from different locations. Also, I know it was always a concern that a dog would get drowned. And of course, it is a frightening thing when a dog and a coon are fighting in the water. I always heard and believed that a coon could/would drown a dog. However, over all the years I don't personally know of an actual dog drowning. Do you personally know of someone who has had one drowned? I certainly believe it is possible, but from my observation a raccoon is more interested in getting away from a dog than in drowning one. Of course, the problem is dropping one in a river and then getting your dog to retrieve the raccoon.

QUESTION

I have a five-month-old walker coonhound that I started training with coon scent almost the week after I got him. He began to do well almost immediately and he was tracking my most complicated scent drags within a few months. By the time he was four months old, he was tracking a drag and treeing the drag in trees. It is now winter. Ace, my dog, recently got in an accident. He got his hind right leg caught in his door flap and his leg lost circulation. It will probably need to be amputated. The point of this question is to ask you about the success a three-legged coon hound can have. I saw a three-legged hound on your web site (the dog named Andy) and I thought maybe you could give me some advice. I hate to give up on the dog if there is a chance for him to still be a good hunter. Thank you for your time.

Lakai

ANSWER

Lakai,

Sorry to hear about your dog. There is still hope for your dog, but he won't be able to advance to the degree he would have with four legs.

The true story on the next page titled "A Three Legged Coonhound" is excerpted from *Devotions for Dog Lovers*.

Bob Rakow with three-legged Andy and
a night's haul of raccoon.

A Three-Legged Coonhound

Andy was "special"—he had three legs. However, he
wasn't born that way. Andy's lifestyle-change took place
when many would have considered him to be middle-
aged.

It happened one evening in a Wisconsin wood while
he was in hot pursuit of a raccoon. Andy climbed a tree
which was hanging out over a steep hillside. Then, at-
tempting to turn around on a limb, he fell. All in all, Andy
dropped some thirty feet. He broke one of his legs which
eventually had to be amputated.

You see, Andy was a purebred bluetick coonhound. For the most part, he had always been a "silent
trailer"—meaning that he limited his voice on the
trail. Indeed, Andy surprised a lot of raccoon. However,
after his accident this all changed.

Andy was frequently allowed the privilege of a soli-
tary run (often he was physically unable to handle much

more than this). In the course of time, Andy converted. Out of necessity he became an "open trailer." This older dog somehow learned that in order to put a coon up a tree, he had to break his silence. Instead of speed, he started depending on the sound of his voice. Yes, to get what he wanted required change. The fact is, if a three-legged coonhound can recognize the need for change, so should we!

More importantly, Jesus told His disciples that change was not only possible, it was actually a prerequisite for getting a foot in heaven. He firmly stated, "I tell you the truth, unless you change and become like little children, you will never enter the kingdom of heaven" (Matthew 18:3). To be a follower of Jesus Christ requires change. Have you changed? With God's help it is possible for anyone to change.

Excerpt—*Devotions for Dog Lovers* by Dr. Tom C. Rakow

THE COAT

For more than half a century, my dad successfully hunted raccoon. Indeed, it's no exaggeration when I say that he spent literally thousands of nights under star-studded skies.

He not only had a passion for the solitude of a late night hunt, but also for the interruption of that same solitude with the sound of a hound either hot on a trail or barking at the tree.

I guess it's only natural that a houndsperson and their dog come to have a unique relationship. Although my dad seldom babied his hounds, he did love them. He took care of them. And we had good dogs. Dogs that were straight. By this I mean that they ran raccoon—and nothing else.

Even so, there were a few times when he would temporarily lose one. It didn't happen often, but it did happen. Usually it was on a windy night when the rattling of cornstalks hampered hearing them. Sometimes they were treeing on the other side of a steep hill or somewhere in a secluded brushy hollow.

When a dog was gone too long on a run, you could sense in Dad's voice both his confidence and concern. Confidence that the hound was on a raccoon and concern that the dog was either caught in a fence or perhaps some other hunter had picked up the dog.

On those rare occasions when a dog did have to be left behind until morning, my dad always did something before we left. Dad would take his jacket off and spread it out on the ground. If there was a cornfield nearby where we had initially parked the truck, he would take the coat in a couple of rows and make a comfortable nest. When Dad returned early the next morning, he would find the dog either curled up on the coat or still at the tree. Yes, Dad's hounds knew where they would find the one who loved them and would take care of them.

In a similar way, God has also left something behind for us as humans so that we can be reunited with our Master. He left it in the Bible. It's not a garment, but rather something far greater. Namely, a wide trail of prophetic passages. Information that has the power to convince and lead a person who is honestly searching for truth into a personal relationship with God's Son—the Lord Jesus Christ.

Indeed, God purposely provided the world with a sacred stream of futuristic truth—a brook of revelation regarding the One whom Hebrew prophets and priests longed to see. A river that continued to flow deeper and wider with the passing of each century until its final fulfillment in Christ.

You see, in our Bibles there exist literally scores of Scriptures which foretold such things as: where the Christ would be born (Micah 5:2), that the child's mother would be a virgin (Isaiah 7:14), as well as the murderous decision of Herod after Christ's birth to have all the baby boys in the vicinity of Bethlehem killed (Jeremiah 31:15).

In addition, the Old Testament writings also predicted the Messiah's ministry (Isaiah 61:1-2), abandonment by His disciples (Zechariah 13:7), casting of lots for Christ's clothes (Psalm 22:18), the piercing of His side with a spear (Zechariah 12:10), and the resurrection of His body (Psalm 16:8-11) just to name a few.

What it really comes down to is this: if a person is looking for someone who really cares for them, the answer is to be found in the Bible. Yes, the answer is found in the person of Jesus Christ who said regarding Himself, "The Son of Man came to seek and to save what was lost" (Luke 19:10). After all, if coonhounds know where to find their master—so should we!

Excerpt—*Devotions for Dog Lovers* by Dr. Tom C. Rakow.

IT WAS A DARK AND STORMY NIGHT

It was a dark and stormy night (it really was!) and I was raccoon hunting alone on the backside of our Wisconsin dairy farm. The dogs ran a raccoon out of a corn strip and took it around the hill. Queenie and Penny (two of our blueticks) were soon treeing hard a couple hundred yards away on top the neighbor's ridge.

However, I just couldn't make my seventeen-year-old legs make that trek to the tree. There was nothing hindering me physically. All I had to do was cross one rusty barbed-wire fence, go through an old cemetery. . . . But wait, that was the problem. There was something inside of me that just would not let me cross that fence and step into the graveyard. It was an old, tiny place of internment and I was familiar with the headstones that marked the hand full of people buried there. In fact, during the daylight hours I had crossed through the middle of that cemetery many times. Nevertheless, doing it on a dark and stormy night just seemed too spooky! Indeed, fear had taken over. So, instead of traveling some 200 yards to the tree, I walked about 500 yards back to the farm buildings.

After arriving back at the house, I eventually talked my girlfriend (who was visiting with my family while I hunted) into hopping in the car with me and retrieving the dogs from a road located on the other side of where they were treeing. I remember I said something like this to her, "Come on, you need to experience this!" But the truth of the matter was that I was afraid to go alone.

How about you? What are you afraid of? If we are willing to admit it, we all either have been, or presently are, afraid of something.

Multitudes are now terrified of terrorism, while still others fear such diverse things as: heights, bats, snakes, showing emotion, spiders, crowds, being left alone, open places, death, and even dirty restrooms. Some fears are healthy and help protect us from harm. The Bible says, "The fear of the Lord is a fountain of life" (Proverbs 14:27a). However, many fears are unhealthy and can either prevent or cripple us from living the kind of life God desires.

King David is often remembered as being a fearless fighter. He not only took on a bear, lion, and an experienced warrior named Goliath while still a youth (1 Samuel 17), but David's entire life was marked with dangerous battles. Was he ever afraid when facing these life and death situations? Sure he was! However, the Bible tells us that when King David experienced fear he chose to combat his fear with faith. David told the Lord, "When I am afraid, I will trust in you" (Psalm 56:3). The presence and power of God was his comfort. David said, "Even though I walk through the valley of the shadow of death, I will fear no evil, for you are with me" (Psalm 23:4). If we have God in our life—there is no need to be afraid. Like David, we too can choose to combat our fears (even a fear of death) with faith in the living God!

Excerpt—*Devotions for Hunters and Anglers* by Dr. Tom C. Rakow.

Bob Rakow pictured with three-legged Andy (his favorite hound of all time), and Baldy.

THE LIFE OF A RACCOON HUNTER

Bob Rakow was born into a family where both parents were totally deaf. Perhaps this is part of the reason he literally loved hearing his hounds on the trail and at the tree. The youngest of six children, Bob was born in 1926 in Clyde, Wisconsin. During the difficult days of the Great Depression his mother told him that they could no longer afford to feed him—and that he should go and ask the neighbors if he could live with them. It was a cold winter night when eight-year-old Bob (with a little sack of clothes) knocked on the neighbor's door. The Browns became his second family and Bob worked for his keep. He paid for his clothing and other personal needs by trapping skunks and hunting raccoon.

Following his service in the Navy during WWII he married his wife Marie who was understanding of his passion to hunt raccoon into the wee hours of the morning. Bob dairy farmed during the day and in the fall, and even early winter, managed to coon hunt about every night. His entire fifty years of raccoon hunting took place among the hardwood-covered hills and corn-stripped valleys of south central Wisconsin.

Over the years, Bob hunted raccoon with a vast variety of dogs. In fact, as a young man his first "coonhound" was a springer spaniel named Rusty. Rusty put up ringneck pheasants during the day and treed raccoon at night. Before he settled on blueticks, his dogs included crosses and even a rat terrier and German shepherd who worked as a team. The terrier trailed and treed while the shepherd served as a kill dog.

In the early 1960's Bob and farming neighbor Larry Weitzel went in together and purchased a female redtick from Arkansas. Kate was a good coon dog, but was later stolen off the chain. However, Bob eventually purchased a young bluetick female that became the basis for years of future hunting stock. Queenie was trained from scratch and was taught to run only raccoon. Indeed, all Bob's blueticks were trained to be straight. When they opened their mouth, you could be certain that they were running raccoon and nothing else. Although he never ran a dog in a night hunt or field trial, he was well known for having truly excellent dogs.

His favorite dog of all time was a bluetick male named Andy. Andy was a silent trailer who kept quiet on the trail, but barked with a great voice on the tree. He caught a lot of coon on the ground. However, Andy had a bad habit of climbing trees. One night shortly after he reached his prime, he treed a coon on a steep side hill. Andy had climbed a leaning hollow tree and chased the coon right past the hole. He was literally treeing in the tree top. Bob tried to coax him down—but in the process of turning around Andy fell about thirty-five feet. His front leg was broken—and eventually it had to be amputated at the shoulder. Nevertheless, in time Andy was again able to hunt. However, due to his decreased speed he changed to an open trailer and began barking on the trail. He somehow learned that in order to put a coon up he needed to depend on his powerful voice rather than his speed.

There were other dogs as well—but Bob's last dog was a well-bred bluetick named George. George started running and treeing his own coon at six months.

Due to health problems, Bob and his wife Marie eventually found it necessary to move from Wisconsin to Arizona. Bob had been a cigarette smoker for decades and the smoking had taken its toll. The Arizona climate caused his health to improve significantly, but his raccoon hunting days were now over.

In 1997 Bob and son Tom began answering questions regarding raccoon hunting on the Rock Dove Publications website www.rockdove.com. They soon began receiving requests for a book from their website readers. So, in 1998 they co-wrote a concise little booklet titled *Raccoon Hunting Basics* which was designed to help the new hunter get started in the sport. *Raccoon Hunting Basics* gave some basic information on getting your dog to tree, conducting a simulated hunt, and tips for keeping your dog on the right track. Since then a much more comprehensive audio tape called *Raccoon Hunting Questions* has also been developed and now the new more extensive book *Raccoon Hunting Basics and Beyond*.

In 1998 Bob was diagnosed with lung cancer. This time of illness resulted in his making a deeper commitment to Jesus Christ and he experienced great peace. Just days before his going to heaven he was still missing his hounds and the hunt. It was especially noticeable that whenever he began talking about Andy he would start to cry. He left this world on August 22, 1998 in Mesa, Arizona. He is survived by his wife Marie, sons Tom and Kelly, daughter Deb, and eight granddaughters.

Bob's vast knowledge of how to train a dog to hunt raccoon continues to help both new and experienced raccoon hunters alike through the Rock Dove Publications website and his written and recorded materials.

SOME RACCOON HUNTING TERMS

Below are some of the terms that are frequently used in relation to raccoon hunting. This list is in no way exhaustive. Furthermore, the terms listed and the definitions that follow should not be understood as being exact or conclusive in their meaning. In some parts of the country or with different hunters they may take on a different shade of meaning. In some instances an entirely different word may be used to convey the definition of a term listed here. Nevertheless, these terms as they are defined here have been used by many hunters over the years.

Baying—This involves your dog(s) barking after having caught or cornered a raccoon. The raccoon will sometimes turn to fight, but will normally seek an opportunity to escape by fleeing to a den or climbing a nearby tree.

Check In—This refers to what a dog does when he or she has been ranging out away from the hunter, and then comes back briefly after a period of time.

Cold Track—When the scent is not as strong due to an extended period of time (perhaps a few hours) which has lapsed before the dog comes in contact with the raccoon's trail. A dog on a cold track may not bark until they have gotten closer to the raccoon.

Hot Track—As opposed to a cold track the scent is strong due to the recent presence of the raccoon or because of favorable tracking conditions (e.g. the grass or forest leaves are damp).

Open Trailer—A dog that normally, if not always, barks on the trail when in pursuit of a raccoon.

Silent Trailer—A dog that either barks very seldom, or not at all on the trail. Indeed, a silent trailer may bark very well at the tree, but not on the trail. Silent trailers frequently catch a significant number of raccoon on the ground.

Simulated Hunt—A hunt which normally involves a trail laid by using raccoon scent, a hide, or a lead raccoon. It is a trail that a dog can follow as a means of eventually developing the dog's ability to track and tree raccoon.

Tapping Tree—There are occasions when a dog will let out a bark, or a few barks at a tree before actually settling down and confidently treeing where the raccoon has gone up. In fact, even the most experienced coon dog will sometimes "tap a tree." This seems to happen for a number of reasons. Sometimes a raccoon may start up a tree and then come back down before going up another tree. Or, the dog may just be making sure that the trail does not continue on. There might also be more than one raccoon in the area.

Trash—For the raccoon hunter this refers to any creature other than a raccoon that your dog chases. For example, if your dog runs a deer or a rabbit they are running trash.

Tree, Treeing, or Treed—This is what takes place when your dog has gotten on a track and chased it to a tree or other location such as an old building or rock den and the dog keeps barking. Getting your dog to bark at the appropriate tree and then to continue barking until you arrive is key.

Rock Dove Publications Order Form

___ *"Copy Me!" Bible Quizzes
(Twenty Reproducible Quizzes!)*: $19.95

___*Messianic Psalms: An Inductive Bible Study*: $5.95

___*Devotions for Dog Lovers*: $7.95

___*Hunting and the Bible: A Scripture Safari*: $3.95

___*Self-Inflicted Hunting Arguments*: $12.95

___*Devotions for Hunters and Anglers*: $14.95

___*The Prodigal Pooch* Tract (pack of 100): $8.95

___*Raccoon Hunting Questions* (audio tape): $9.95

___*Raccoon Hunting Basics and Beyond*: $14.95

Shipping free in the USA. Otherwise add $2. Minnesota residents add 6.5% tax.

1) Call toll-free 1-888-HIS-DOVE.
2) Order online at http://www.rockdove.com
3) Mail this form with name, address, and payment to:
   Rock Dove Publications
   PO Box 203
   Silver Lake, MN 55381

TOTAL ENCLOSED_____